Grant Writing Basics

Dr. Ponchitta Young

Kindle Direct Publishing
ISBN- 13: 979-8-218-53299-4

Library of Congress Publication Data

Author: Dr. Ponchitta Young

This book is dedicated to those who have a sincere passion to serve and create opportunities for change.

Table of Contents:

Introduction

Do you have a passion to change something, or to help resolve a problem? You may desire to help minimize homelessness; provide housing opportunities for single mothers; offer medical treatment for homeless pets; medical equipment for seniors; or create a mentoring program for the youth. Whatever your passion may be, it takes money to have your goal fulfilled.

It may be a cliché, but were you born with a gold or silver spoon in your mouth? Or perhaps your family have the kind of money that never ends. It would be awesome if any of these were true. Unfortunately, rarely is this a realistic position for many of us. It's interesting how the desire to do or commit good toward others is oftentimes beyond our reach unless external support is available. Money, yes! money is what you need. Not only do you need money, but you need the right connections to help support your vision to create transformation for something or someone else, and to solve a problem. Remember, your vision did not appear because you ate something indifferent the night before or saw a horror movie and suddenly became scared straight. You are passionate about what you believe, how you feel, what you see, and the impact or the lack thereof residing within your community. Your passion is leading you to do something about it.

Grant Writing Basics is designed to educate, motivate, and offer strategies to assist you in obtaining resources needed to solve a problem. Your nonprofit organization, whether community, faith-based, etc., cannot operate without consistent funds available to meet the demands of the problem you are trying to solve. Grant Writing Basics will teach you how to structure a well written grant request. This book is intended to provide very **basic** knowledge of grant writing.

As you read through Grant Writing Basics, focus strongly on your program's mission, vision and the need you want to meet. Let's talk about your purpose for wanting to see change. Don't allow lack of money, connections, education, or skills to hinder the manifestation of this significant change. Thoughts and ideas you have shared with others will never go away until you put those thoughts into action. These heartfelt thoughts were ignited intentionally to create a much-needed cycle of change for many generations to come.

Chapter 1

What is Grant Money?

Grant money is a sum of money given by the government or other organizations for a particular purpose. **https://www.collinsdictionary.com**
Grant money is free money; it does not have to be paid back. However, you must consider the purpose and guidelines in which grant money is given. If the guidelines are not adhered to, the grantor may request the money to be returned due to non-compliance or forfeiture of agreement.
The ***grantor*** is the entity who provides grant funding. The ***grantee*** is the recipient. The grantor outlines specific guidelines or an agreement regarding the use of the funds. It is so important to follow these guidelines. Later we will discuss a component in this process called Grant Management.

Your request for grant funds needs to be precise. Before writing a grant request make sure the request is in sync with your organization's mission and vision. If not, STOP! do not apply for this grant. Your money chasing scheme will be discovered, and the application could possibly be denied almost immediately. Remember, you want your organization to remain credible throughout the community and with grantors. When writing grants, time management is vital. Do not spend unnecessary time trying to force an unassigned mission and vision.

Figure 1 gives an example of the phase we hear often, "mission creep or mission drift." When this happens, your mission is no longer intentional with its original purpose. **http://www.fundingforgood.org**

Figure 1.

Org.	Cycle	Mission	Funding category/ amount	$ spent	Funds used for	balance	Agr. Met ?
AB	Jan.- Dec.	Education	$30,000 Education (supplies, 1 FT staff, marketing	$30,000	Education	$0	Yes
XY	Jan.- Dec.	Mental health services to 100 clients	$50,000 Nutrition (purchase food)	$50,000	Office supplies, travel, payroll	$0	No

Did you notice how organization XY utilized their funds. The organization's mission is related to mental health. They managed to convince the grantor of a nutrition program, and used the funds to purchase supplies, support travel and payroll. What problems do you see? After reviewing figure 1, your response should be: #1. XY organization shifted their mission to accommodate the criteria of the grant application. #2. XY organization did not follow the guidelines of the grant; funds were spent on items not agreed upon. It is vital to follow the guidelines of the grant. Grantors will outline funding categories and indicate what funds can and cannot be used for. Whenever in doubt, contact the grantor for clarification. You should never apply for funding in a category that is not consistent with your organization's mission.

Chapter 2

What you need before writing for a grant

A. If you haven't already done so, your organization can apply for an EIN, apply for an approved Non-Profit 501(c)(3) tax exempt code status by Internal Revenue Service. Exempt purposes - Internal Revenue Code Section 501(c)(3) | Internal Revenue Service (irs.gov)
** **check the guidelines of your State regarding corporation registration and charity registration
B. Mission and Vision: Mission (what is your organization's purpose for existing; why are you here); Vision (what is the overall outcome once the mission is achieved; at the end of the day what do you want to see happen)
C. Have a governing Board of Directors: this is not a solo operation; your Board should assist you with how to fulfill the organizations' mission/vision; provide oversight and governance
D. Have a physical location (address) to operate a business: at some point grantors may require a site visit
E. Maintain good record keeping showing the integrity and accountability of your financial

data: Balance Sheet, Financial Statement, Profit & Loss; or an audit report by a Certified Public Accountant

F. An organization and program budget: a financial outline to determine what revenue is received and what the expenses are
G. A Strategic Plan: identify 3-to-5-year organizational goals and objectives highlighting steps to achieve each strategy

Assignment:

Now let's put these strategies in order!

1. B	Know your purpose, who you will serve and the impact: draft the mission/vision and know it well
2. C	Have others committed to assisting in solving the problem- support is necessary
3. D	Identify a location where the business of the organization will take place (you need a physical address)
4. A	Legalize your organization from both State and Federal levels: incorporate the organization, apply for an EIN with IRS; apply for Non-Profit status

5. F	Create a budget: having a snapshot of how you receive and spend money is critical
6. E	Keep good financial records; need to be consistent
7. G	A strategic plan may not necessarily be required for some grantors, but it is important in showing the direction of your organization

How did you do? Although the order of results may vary for some, all these strategies are needed for grant approval. If you are a new nonprofit organization, don't resist attaining legal advice regarding your State and Federal registrations, especially for your 501(c)(3) application. You may be comfortable submitting these documents without support, if so that's great. However, it's ok to seek assistance from a legal expert.

Remember to include these expenses in your budget. *** If your nonprofit organization is not new, track the impact of programs and services you have provided.

Chapter 3

Write a Mission Statement

The mission statement should identify your organization's purpose. ***Please write in pencil, revisions may be needed later***

Mission Statement examples:

1. ABC will minimize housing insecurity in Chase County
2. XYZ will empower children and families to thrive in their existing community

Are you ready? Let's try creating your nonprofit organization's mission statement. Draft the mission statement on the lines below.
Name your organization/what is its purpose, practice, practice, practice

____

____

____

____

____

____

____

____

____

Chapter 4

Write a Vision Statement

The vision statement should identify your achievement/impact. ***(please write in pencil revisions may be needed later)***

Vision Statement examples: (think broad)

1. ABC: Residents of Chase County will not have experience homelessness
2. XYZ: Children and families will no longer live in poverty.

Name your nonprofit organization/what is its intended impact

____

____

____

____

____

____

____

____

____

____

____

____

Great job!!!

Utilize this page to practice more on the mission and vision for your organization. Remember, your mission describes your purpose. The vision should describe the overall impact. Your mission and vision should be brief, but intentional.

Chapter 5

Board of Directors

Have a list of the organizations' Board of Directors, this should include the information below for an odd number of board members selected (an odd number is helpful particularly when a voting process in involved):

A. Name
B. Board position
C. Address
D. Phone number
E. Email address
F. Area of expertise or occupation
G. Time served on the board or number of terms
H. Regularly attend board meetings
I. Contributes gifts to the organization

Utilize this time to establish your organizations' Board of Directors/Members
(please write in pencil, revisions may be needed later)

Chief Executive Officer — *some may use this position also has the board chair*

Chairman or President

Vice President

Secretary

Treasurer/CFO

Additional Members

Here are a few Board resources to reference when organizing your board. Hopefully this will provide greater knowledge about board governance and roles and responsibilities for each board of directors or member. The resource is intended to establish consistent guidelines as the organization pursues meaningful growth opportunities.

- Boardable

https://www.boardable.com

- National Council of Nonprofits

https://www.councilofnonprofits.org

- Foundation Group

https://www.501c3.org/nonprofits-board-directors/

- Internal Revenue Service

https://www.irs.gov/pub/irs-tege/governance_practices.pdf

Chapter 6

Financials

It is important to maintain good financial records for your nonprofit organization. Grantors look for fiscal accountability and great stewardship. At minimum, your financial template should include revenue and expenses. There are several software programs to assist with displaying revenue, expenses, assets, liability, cash flow, balance sheet, profit and loss, and many other categories. Financial statements will highlight the health of your nonprofit organization.

Consider investing in a software program to record all the organization's financial data. There are many available, but here are a few to get you started. While you are reviewing financial software resources, also consider a program that will monitor donor contributions. Donors like to receive a tax deduction document from your organization to file on their tax return.

Here are just a few resources to record financial data:

1. Intuit QuickBooks
2. Quicken
3. Church Windows
4. Servant Keeper

5. Blackbaud
6. Neon One

Documents Needed:
if you have these documents, place a check mark to the right of each

- ✓ 501(c)(3) approval letter
- ✓ State incorporation status letter
- ✓ State charity approval letter (if required)
- ✓ Board of Directors list
- ✓ Mission Statement
- ✓ Vision Statement
- ✓ Program Description
- ✓ Statement of Needs

- ✓ Executive Summary
- ✓ Budget (organization)
- ✓ Budget (each program)
- ✓ Financial Records (use software system)
- ✓ Letters of support (may be required)
- ✓ Attestation form (board approval of financial documents
- ✓ DEI Policy (Diversity, Equity, Inclusion)
- ✓ Reserve Policy (indicates savings account to cover at least 3 months of the organization's expenses
- ✓ Human Resource Policy
- ✓ Identify the population served
- ✓ Strategic Plan
- ✓ Donor list and award amounts

- ✓ Tax return (990 or 990 EZ)

- ✓ Overhead calculation (should not exceed 25 to 30%)

This is a very basic list to get you started. Some grantors may require additional documentation and statements such as: Social Justice statement; political statement (whether your organization endorse/support political views). Not all these documents are needed, but please remember as your organization grows and pursues higher funding levels, more information may be required.

It is always best to prepare earlier rather than later. It is important to familiarize yourself with these documents and consider them the best fit for your organization.

Chapter 7

Partnerships

Partnerships are a must. The organization's leadership team needs to initiate partnerships through solid, meaningful connections. Great connections will set the tone for great relationships. A few connections may include your elected officials, local foundations, other nonprofit organizations, civic groups, local business, churches, schools, neighbors, sororities, and fraternities.

As you build upon these connections, one great relationship shares the value of the relationship with another, and suddenly your domino effect may produce more funding opportunities. The process of building relationships: **Consistently** show up with purpose, say something intentional, and do something with passion and integrity.

Show up:	Be visible and supportive as often as possible
Say something:	Your language must be in sync with all partnerships' mission/interest/passion, and your organization

Do something:	Utilize your skills and knowledge for good to provoke positive change (help to resolve the problem; collaborate)
Use Integrity:	Integrity sets the tone for lasting partnerships- it speaks value to the organizations' leadership

Visibility is critical; attend scheduled meetings and events as much as possible. Stay connected to local news outlets, articles, and other publications within your community; this will increase your knowledge base. As you attend meetings of such, your input and or observation will become significant and ultimately benefit the organization.

Identify current or potential partnerships for our organization:

1. ____
2. ____
3. ____
4. ____
5. ____
6. ____
7. ____

As you utilize the template for practice, you will become more and more comfortable with the process. Grant writing requires a lot of writing. Identify someone or an electronic application software to proofread the narrative portions of your grant. Read your grant application at least three to four times, ensuring accuracy of the information and documents you have presented.

You are ready to apply for a grant!!! Look at the next few pages to view a sample grant template.

Chapter 8

Grant Application Template

<u>XXX Foundation</u>

We provide funding opportunities for nonprofit organizations with an approved 501(c)(3) code status by Internal Revenue Services. We support the missions of building capacity for human service needs. Our grant funding awards range from $10,000 to $25,000. Our application deadline is January 5, 2025, by 4:00pm. Our reviewers will decide regarding all funding applications no later than March 15, 2025. Submissions may be submitted electronically or 3 copies by mail to: XYZ 002 First St. Cesa, Tonto 00320.

Organization name:
Mailing Address, to include city, state, and zip code:
Phone number:
Email:
Website address:

Leadership:

Executive Director name and contact

Board Chairman name and contact

EIN: ____________________

Year incorporated: ______________

Do you have a governing Board of Directors ______ yes ______no

Are you using a fiscal sponsor for this proposal? Fiscal Sponsors are generally used by organizations who do not yet have their own 501(c)(3) charitable status. Perhaps you have a fiscal agent who will monitor funds received until your charitable status is approved, if this is true for your organization, your answer would be YES; if you do not have fiscal sponsorship and have your own 501(c)(3), your answer would be NO

Organization's Mission Statement:

This should be a one to two sentence summary of your organization's purpose.

Amount Requesting: ___________________

Who do you serve? (500 words maximum, please be sure to include demographics)

Please identify the diversity of your organization: (staff and board members)
Race/Ethnicity (300 word maximum)

What is your primary focus: religion, human service, education, training, disaster, healthcare, political (Please keep in mind, we do NOT endorse religious or political views or support for funding)

____

Organization Budget ___________________

Program Budget _______________________

Name your program project:

____

Tell us about your organization's previous activities related to your funding request: (1,000 word maximum)

Identify Key Partners for your project:

Are you currently receiving funding for this project, if so by whom, how much, and when was it received

Statement of Needs: (minimum 300 words, maximum 500 words)

Program/project description: (minimum 300 words, maximum 500 words)

What is your expected impact for this project? (1,000 word maximum):

How do plan to measure the success of your project?

What applications, software programs, and other systems you plan to use for this project?

Do you have a Diversity, Equity and Inclusion Policy? If so, please provide a copy

Does your organization have a Reserve Policy? If so, please provide a copy

Conclusion: (use this space to share additional information about your project)

What is the best method of contact: email ______ or phone _______

Please provide copies of the following documents: for the current year

Budgets (org. and program)

financial statements or (audit if available)

P & L (profit & loss)

Balance Sheet

990 or 990 EZ (previous year)

Board of Director's List

A template of your measurement tool

Although it is not required feel free to share photos and or success stories of your organization's activities related to this project

Executive Director's Signature:

____

Date Submitted:

____

YOU DID IT!!

Chapter 9

Grant Management

Grant management is the required process which ensures compliance and impact of the grant. For example, if a grantor requires a six-month report, data within this timeframe must be submitted. The report may include the number of clients served, benchmarks (current impact), and financial data to show the spenddown of specific budget items.

Grant management can be captured on any application of your choice. Microsoft Excel, Access, or Word platforms can be used depending on the intensity of your program requirements. Some grantors may provide a grant management template. If a template is not received, your organization should establish one. We have provided a basic template to use for grant management reporting.

Grant Management 6-month Reporting

Funding Category:	Education
Funding Amount:	$10,000
Date received:	01/02/2025
Program Goal:	50% of students enrolled will achieve at reading grade level
Tools used:	academic reporting; pre/post-reading assessment

Program: Education- (Reading Academy)

Date assessed	Name of student	Student's grade	Prior reading level	Current reading level (6 months)	Impact met
6/2/25	Jane Doe	4	3	4.7	Yes; 1.7 rate gain
6/4/25	Jon Doe	2	2	2.8	Yes; .8 rate gain
6/15/25	Sue Doe	6	4	4.2	No; some gain but not met
6/23/25	Becky Doe	5	4	4.4	No; some gain but not met

Number of students: 4
Number of students reading on grade level or above: 2
% of reading rate improvement: 50%

Financials:

Please attached a 6-month financial statement for this program (ex: profit and loss showing itemization of income and expenses)

The objective of Grant Writing Basics was to provide simple strategies to complete a grant application successfully. Grant writing can become very complex as funding requests increase. With a few good tips and information previously provided, you are on your way to receiving the funding needed for your program.

Final Tips:

- Always proofread your work
- Keep at least two hardcopies of your grant application
- Keep your copies easily accessible (in a binder, file cabinet)
- Save your electronic copy on your PC in a special folder; name the folder according to the grantor or specific program
- Create your grant management template and monitor it closely
- Monitor the budget
- As your impact increase seek additional funding opportunities
- Stay engaged with the Board of Directors, partners, clients, and anyone connected to the success of the program

- Publicize your program success (website, social media outlets, email blast, and many others)
- Obtain success stories, thank you notes, and photos as often as possible
- Always seek to improve the work of the organization and in all program areas

Made in the USA
Columbia, SC
17 February 2025

53980579R00024